A Day
of our Own

Liam Lawton

A Day of our Own

Music for a Wedding Liturgy

VERITAS

Published 2004 by
Veritas Publications
7/8 Lower Abbey Street
Dublin 1
Ireland
Email publications@veritas.ie
Website www.veritas.ie

ISBN 1 85390 880 0

Liam Lawton would like to thank
Colette Dower, Joan O'Neill and all at Veritas Publications, Dublin
and GIA Publications Inc., Chicago.

A Day of our Own is also available on CD.

Cover design by Colette Dower
Music setting by Matthew Hébert
Origination by Digital Prepress Imaging
Printed in the Republic of Ireland by Betaprint, Dublin

Veritas books are printed on paper made from the wood pulp of managed forests. For every tree felled, at least one tree is planted, thereby renewing natural resources.

CONTENTS

INTRODUCTION

This collection of music for your wedding day has been drawn from a number of my published collections and it is my hope that you will find this a helpful resource in choosing music for your special day. The Christian wedding ceremony is about gathering in God's presence with family and friends to invoke God's sacramental blessing on your lives together. There are many elements of this liturgical celebration and music can greatly enhance the occasion. Today there are many resources to chose from, but all too often we limit ourselves to what we already know or have already heard at other weddings in the past. This collection is an opportunity to praise God in a new way.

One question that continually arises concerns the use of secular music – non religious music – in our wedding services and whether or not this is permissible. I would like to think that when we gather in Church we are there to express our faith and belief in God and in Jesus Christ. If the music that I use will do this then it is wholly appropriate. Very often couples may wish to use some beautiful love songs that may be special to them with many memories. However I would suggest that such songs might be used later, outside of the liturgical celebration. God has blessed us with many gifts and is present in a very special way in the sacrament of marriage. It is thus fitting that we should give God thanks and praise when we come together to pray for His blessing. This praise is not only through our words, but also in our songs.

The music listed in this collection is divided into the various elements of the Mass with choices within each section. This allows the couple to make suggestions and choices for themselves. The book is accompanied by a CD recording to help in these choices. This music can also be used for wedding celebrations where Mass is not celebrated, for example in an interfaith marriage.

It would be a pity to leave the choice of music merely to those who are responsible for providing the music. It is you, the couple whose wedding it is, who should choose the music with the help of those who are involved with the music ministry. It is a good idea to talk about your choices and discuss these with the priest or minister who is officiating at the wedding. Why not encourage the family and friends gathered for the wedding to join in the singing? You can do this by asking the Cantor or the Soloist to invite all to participate and also by providing the words in your wedding booklet or on a separate sheet if you are not using a booklet. If people are encouraged to be involved they will respond.

Music is full of memory and I hope and believe that using this music will enhance your special day – a day in which family and friends can be mere spectators or members of the family of God who gather to express their faith and belief and invoke God's blessing on two very special people at a very special moment in their lives. May they, and you, do so with a song in your hearts and a prayer on your lips.

Liam Lawton

HOLY IS GOD

Words and Music by Liam Lawton
Arranged by John McCann

Lively ♩ = 95

Introduction

Verses

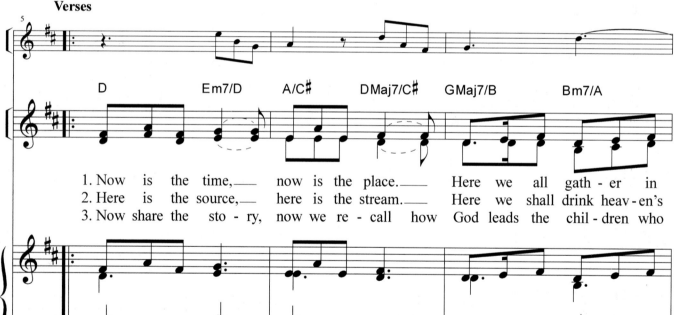

1. Now is the time,___ now is the place.___ Here we all gath-er in
2. Here is the source,___ here is the stream.___ Here we shall drink heav-en's
3. Now share the sto-ry, now we re-call how God leads the chil-dren who

All you who hun - ger, come seek and find_____
All who de - spair,_____ come from the night._____
Let us give praise,_____ let us de - light._____

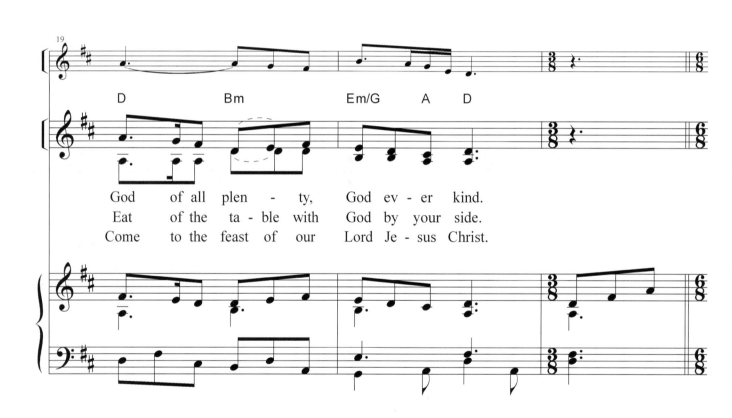

God of all plen - ty, God ev - er kind.
Eat of the ta - ble with God by your side.
Come to the feast of our Lord Je - sus Christ.

PSALM 95: SING A SONG TO THE LORD

Words and Music by Liam Lawton
Arranged by John McCann

Last time to Coda ⊕

14

Verses

Em · A · D/F# · Em · Em/G

1. Give the Lord, you fam-'lies of peo-ple,—— Give the Lord—— glo-ry and
2. Tell the world our God rules with jus-tice.—— Tell the world its prais-es to
3. Day by day we count on God's bless-ings.—— Day by day we seek for God's

Asus4 · A · Em · A · Bm

pow'r.—— Give the Lord a heart that is grate-ful.—— Let us
sing.—— Tell the world God's peo-ple know fair-ness.—— Let our
strength.—— Day by day may love be our les-son.—— May our

Em · Gadd9 · A7sus4,2 · A · *D.S.*

tell of the glo-ry of God.——
voic-es pro-claim God is King.——
won-der of God have no end.——

D.S.

15

BLEST ARE YOU

Based on Psalm 128

Words and Music by Liam Lawton
Arranged by John Drummond

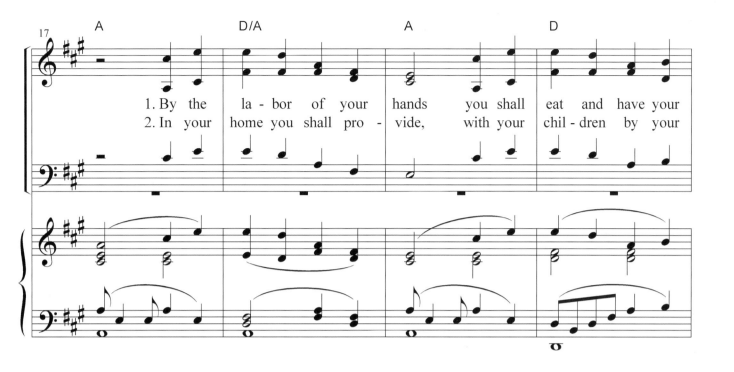

1. By the la - bor of your hands you shall eat and have your
2. In your home you shall pro - vide, with your chil - dren by your

fill. You shall_____ pros - per.
side. Love be_____ your bless - ing.

You shall_____ pros - per.
Love be_____ your bless - ing.

Blest are

Verse 3

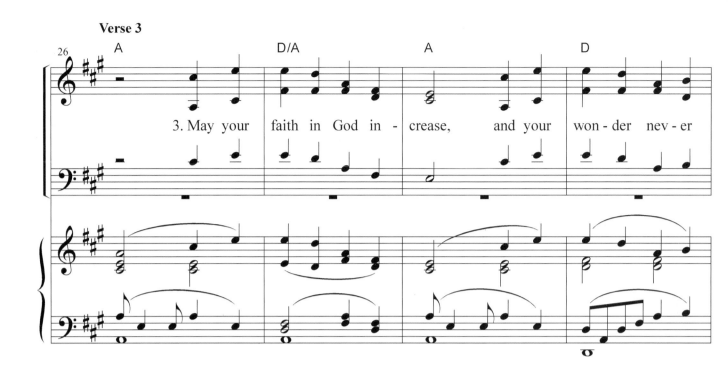

3. May your faith in God in - crease, and your won - der nev - er

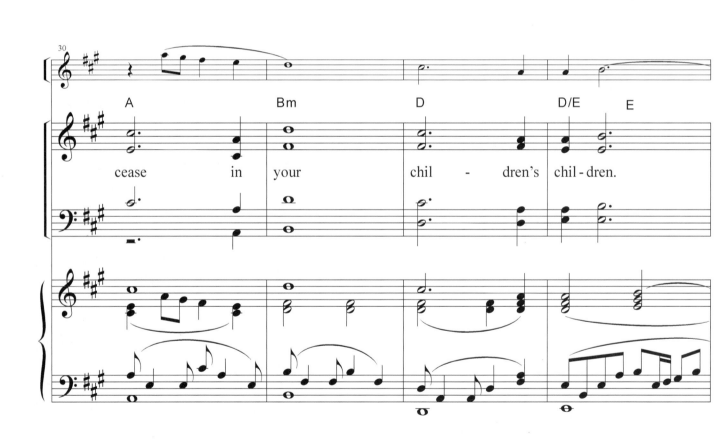

cease in your chil - dren's chil - dren.

Final Refrain

Blest are you who fear the Lord,

Blest are you who walk in God's ways.

HIDING PLACE

Based on Psalm 17

Words and Music by Liam Lawton
Vocal arranged by Gary Daigle

Gently ♩ = 82
Introduction/Coda

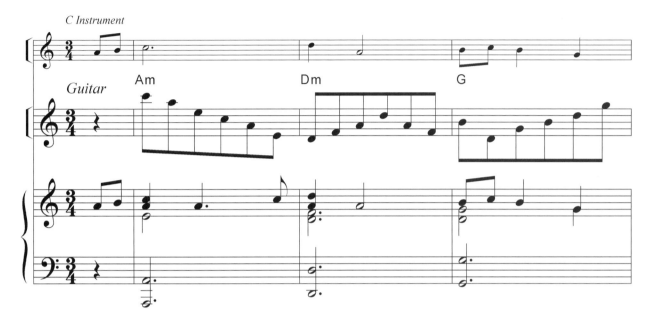

Refrain

a tempo

Descant (after Verse 1)
a tempo

I will search in the si - lence for your hid - ing place. In the

Melody
a tempo

I will search in the si - lence for your hid - ing place. In the

a tempo

quiet, Lord, I seek your face.

quiet, Lord, I seek your face.

si - lence   I   call   out   your   name.
shad - ows   I   long   for   your   light.

Verse 3

Cantor(s)

3. Lead   me in your   foot - steps   a - long   your an-cient   way.   Let me

walk   in   the   love   of   the   Lord.   Your

wis - dom is my heart's wealth, a bless - ing all our days. In the

Oh

si - lence I long for your world.

ah   ah

Final Refrain

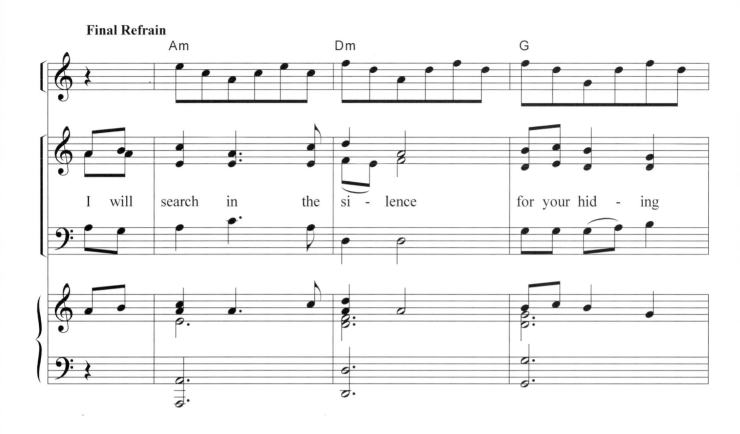

I will search in the si - lence for your hid - ing

place. In the quiet, Lord, I seek your face.

To Optional Coda*

*The Coda is the same as the Introduction.

HOW CAN I REPAY?

Psalm 116

Words and Music by Liam Lawton

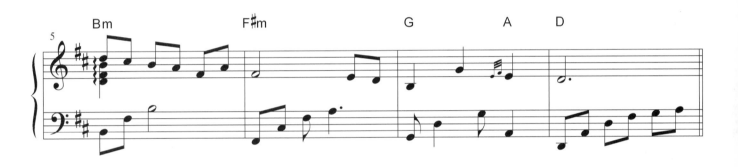

How can I re-pay the Lord for his good-ness to___ me?

29

Fine after final verse

How can I re-pay the Lord for his good-ness to—— me?

1. I will call, I will call, on the Lord's own name, my

2. O Lord, my God,—— your ser-vant am I.

3. I trust, I trust, ev-en when I say, look at

PILGRIM SONG
ALLELUIA

Music by Liam Lawton
Vocal Arrangement by Ian Callanan

♩ = 126

Introduction

33

Verse for Advent Season

Seek the Lord, for his day is near.

Call to him, pre - pare the way.

Seek the Lord, for his day is near. We

wait in ex - pec - ta - tion for the Sav - iour's birth

Verse for Christmas Season

Glo - ry to God in the high - est hea - ven.

Peace to all peo - ple, all peo - ple on earth.

Glo - ry to God in the high - est hea - ven. We

sing in ju - bi - la - tion for the Sav - iour's birth.

Verse for Easter 1

Christ has died, Christ is ris - en.

Christ will come a - gain, will come a - gain.

Christ has died, Christ is ris - en.

Christ the be - gin - ning, Christ the end.

Verse for Easter 2

Glor - ry to God, for his end - less love.

Praise to the Lord, for all that is good.

Glor - ry to God, for his end - less love.

For He has tri - umphed and shall raise us up.

THE WEAVER

Words and Music by Liam Lawton
Piano and Vocal Arrangement by Ian Callanan

Instrumental

2nd Movement

3rd Movement

'SÉ DO BHEATHA MHUIRE

Words and Music by Liam Lawton
Arranged by Julianne Woods

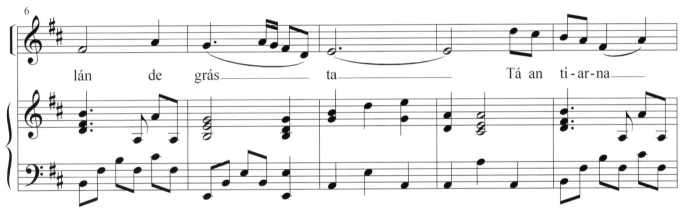

idir mná ——————— a-gus beann ai the tor adh do bhroin-ne

Ío - sa.——————— A Naomh——————— Mhúire,

Mathair——————— Dé——————————————— Guí———

orainn na peac aí a - nois——————— 'gus ar uair ar

mbáis,   A - men,_____   A - - - -

men,_____   A - - - - men._____

PEACE PRAYER

Music by Liam Lawton

I WILL BE THE VINE

Based on John 15

Words and Music by Liam Lawton
Arranged by John McCann

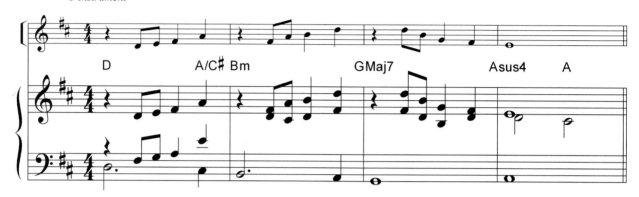

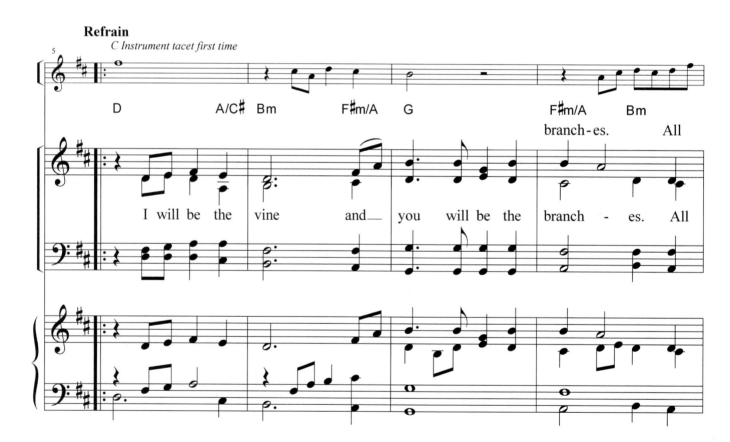

you who live in me will nev - er, nev - er die.

you_____ who live in me will nev - er die._____

I will be the sign, I will of - fer man - y chanc - es; so

I will be the sign, I will of - fer man - y chanc - es; so

I will be the sign, I will of - fer man - y chanc - es; so

COME TO THE FEAST DIVINE

Words and Music by Liam Lawton
Arranged by John Drummond

♩ = 116

Introduction

C Instrument

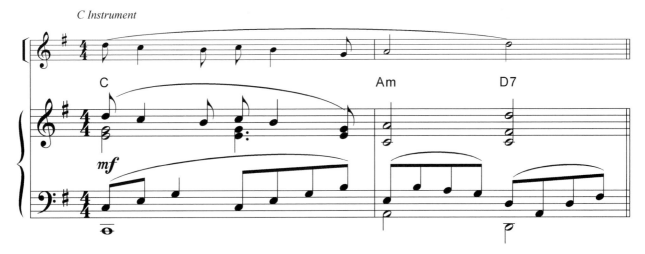

Refrain

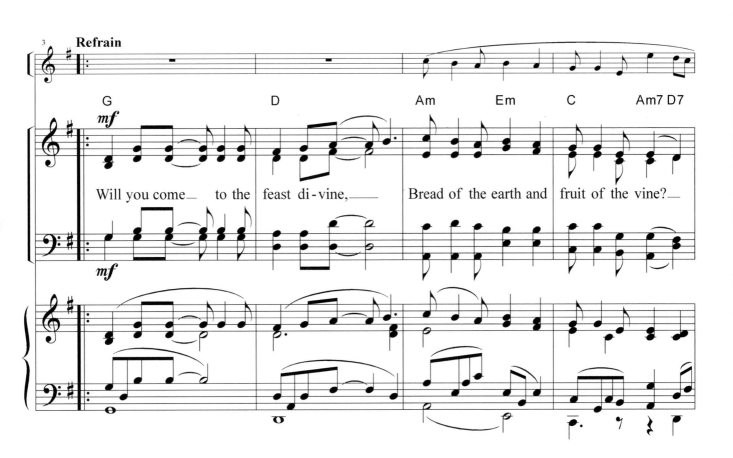

Will you come to the feast di-vine, Bread of the earth and fruit of the vine?

Come and taste— the heav-en-ly wine,— Wel-come the lost and the stran - ger.

Come to the feast of the an - gels.

Verses 1, 2

Bm   C   Am7   D7   C   Em   Am7   D7

1. Make of your hands now a hum-ble cra-dle, As once I came to a hum-ble man-ger.
2. Make of your life a re-newed de-ci-sion, Ban-ish all hate and all heart's di-vi-sion.

G   C   Am7   D7   C

Make of your hearts now a low-ly sta-ble, Love   be
Make of your mind a home for my wis-dom, Truth   be

Let love be,
Let truth be,

55

born a - gain.
born a - gain.

be born a - gain.
be born a - gain.

D   D7

3. Make of our world a place of love's car-ing, Serv-ing and feed-ing, heal-ing and shar-ing.

Bm C Am7 D7 C Em Am7 D7

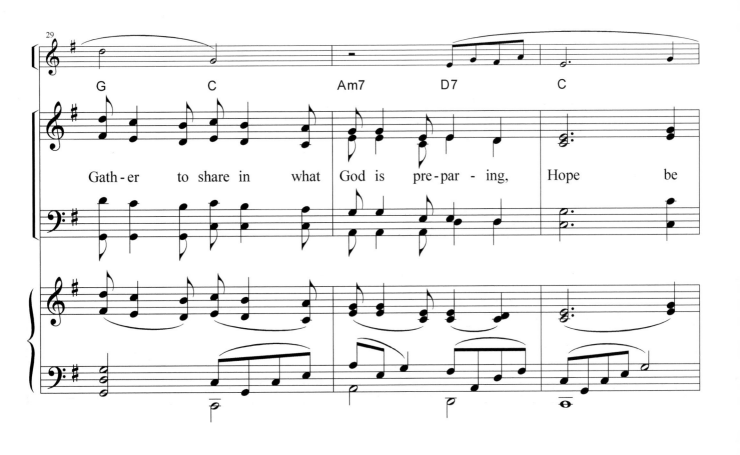

Gath-er to share in what God is pre-par-ing, Hope be

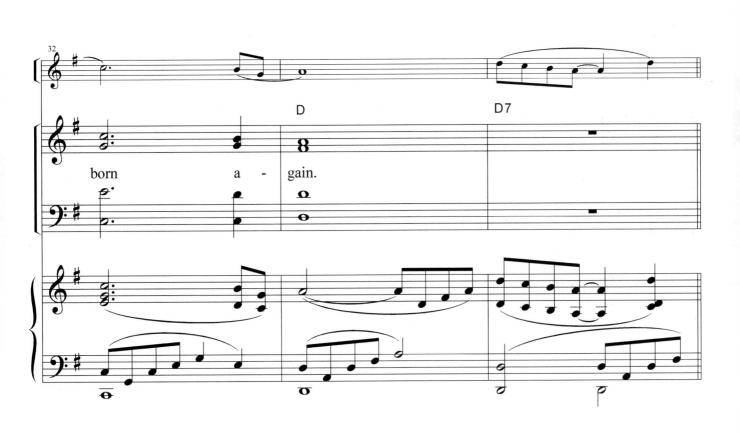

born a - gain.

Final Refrain

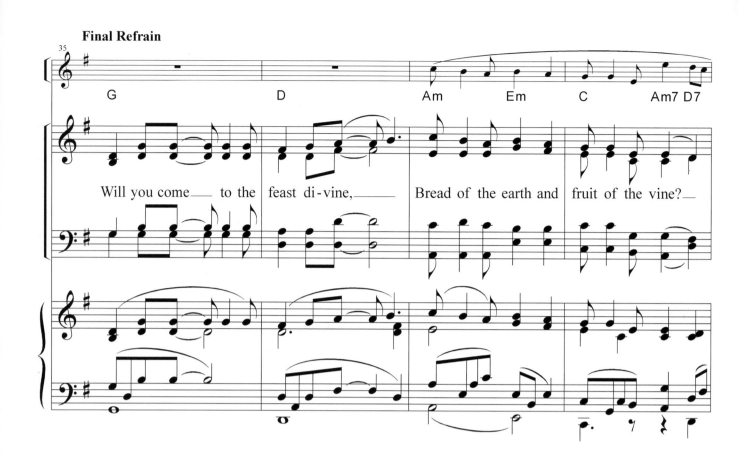

Will you come to the feast di-vine, Bread of the earth and fruit of the vine?

Come and taste the heav-en-ly wine, Wel-come the lost and the stran - ger.

Come to the feast of the an - gels.

WHEN THIS DAY IS DONE

Words and Music by Liam Lawton
Arranged by John Drummond

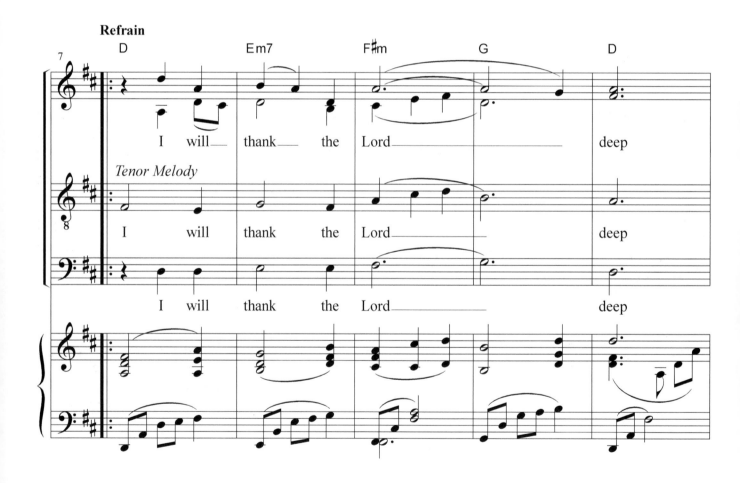

Final Refrain

THE MAGNIFICAT: GLORIFY THE LORD

Based on Luke 1:46-55

Words and Music by Liam Lawton
Arranged by John McCann

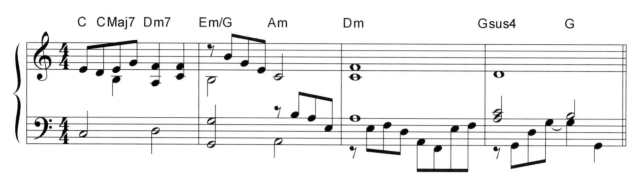

* The Refrain may be used as an alternate Introduction

Refrain

C Instrument: Play only as alternate Introduction

CMaj7 F   G   Am

I will glo - ri-fy ___ the Lord. ___ I will

Glo - ri-fy ___ the Lord. ___

F   G   G/E G7/D CMaj7

glo - ri-fy ___ the Lord. ___

Glo - ri-fy ___ the Lord. ___

Verse 3

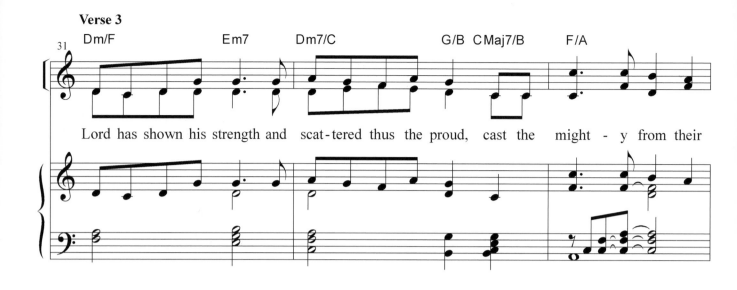

Lord has shown his strength and scat-tered thus the proud, cast the might - y from their thrones.

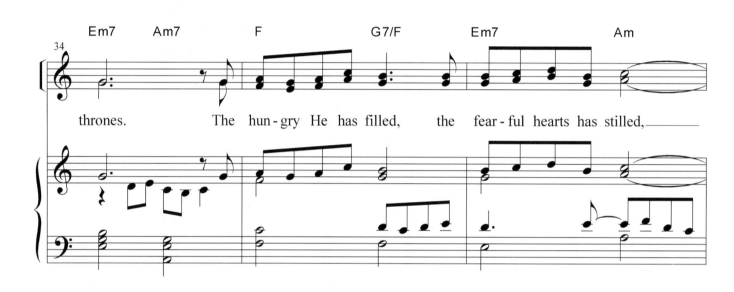

The hun - gry He has filled, the fear - ful hearts has stilled,

To Verse 4

sends the rich and wealth - y ones a - way.

To Verse 4

ON THE JOURNEY

Words and Music by Liam Lawton
Arranged by John McCann

1. On the jour - ney, seek the
2. On the jour - ney, seek - ing
3. On the jour - ney, call all
4. On the jour - ney, bless the

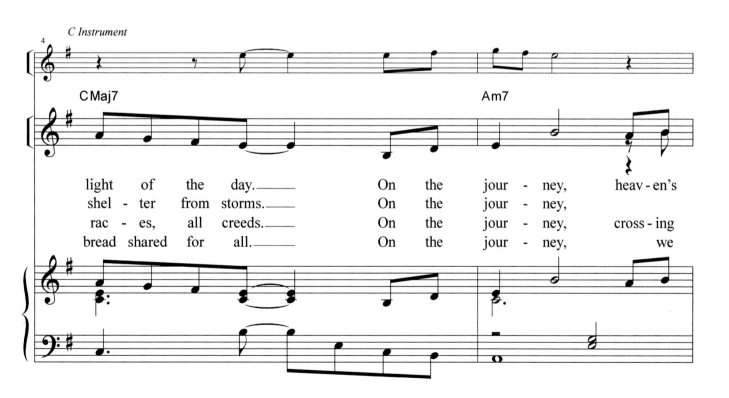

light of the day.___ On the jour - ney, heav - en's
shel - ter from storms.___ On the jour - ney,
rac - es, all creeds.___ On the jour - ney, cross - ing
bread shared for all.___ On the jour - ney, we

let all the world—be-lieve.—— The ris-en Lord— now calls

Last time to Coda

us— to pros-per in— his peace.—

Coda

76

THE CLOUDS' VEIL

Words and Music by Liam Lawton
Arranged by John McCann

77

weep,_____ e - ven in the night when storms shall rise,
weep,_____ e - ven when the storms shall rise,
weep, e - ven when the storms shall rise,

D/A   A   F#m   F#m7/E   Bm7   G

God is by my side. God is by my side.
God is by my side._____ God is by my side.
God is by my side._____ God is by my side.

D/A   A7   GMaj7/B   A7   G9   A7   D

Fine last time

79

THIS IS
SONG OF MICAH

Based on Micah 6:8

Words and Music by Liam Lawton
Arranged by John Drummond

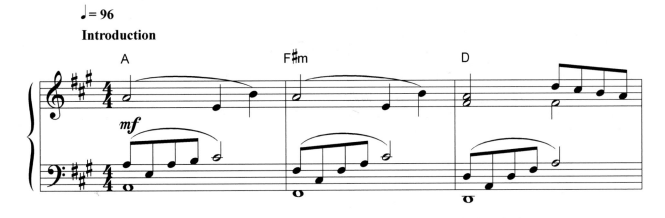

This is, this is what God now asks of you,

Three things,— three things— that I want you to do:—

To act— just-ly,— to love—

Melody

To act just-ly,— to love

ten-der-ly—And to walk hum-bly with— your God.—

Last time To Coda

84

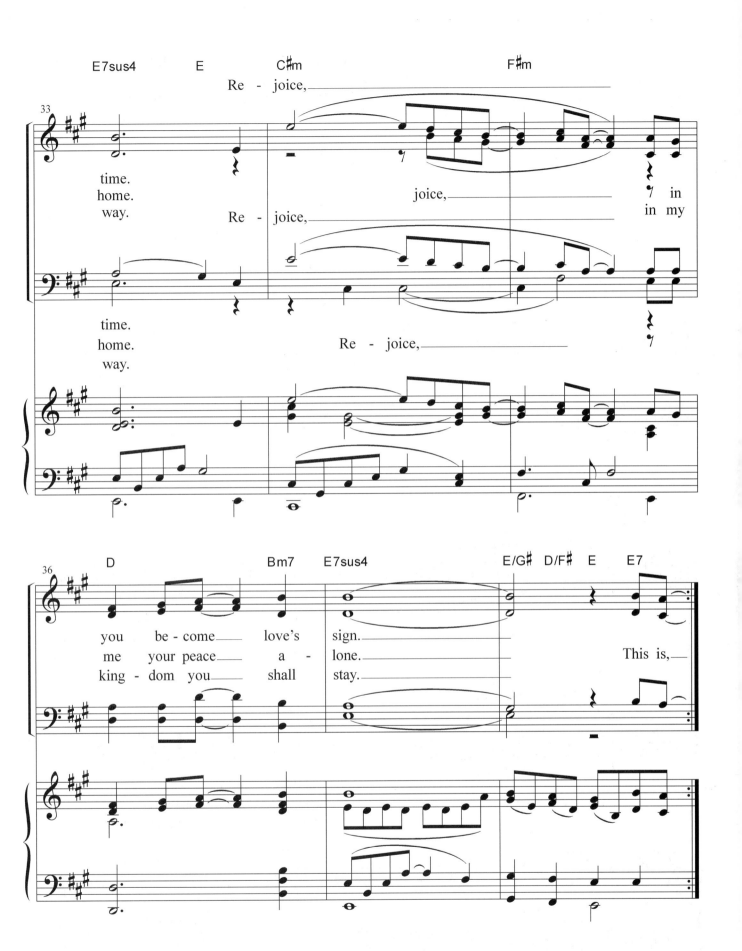

God._____ And to walk hum-bly with__ your God._____